Scribbles

Michael

To L,
It only took seven years and five lives,
but it's yours. It always was.

ˋ

CONTENTS

LAS VEGAS

I want to
build you a place
that doesn't hurt

I'm pretty sure silence
is just her
leaving the world
speechless again

there is something
buried here
in my debris
that knows exactly how
to love you

just loving her isn't enough
show her
write her a poem
bring her a cup of coffee and a flower
make her your morning meditation
it doesn't have to be complicated
but it does have to be something

she lingers on me
like smoke
like everything
I've ever tried to quit
but couldn't

I am defenseless
against things like
coffee
and rain
and her

I've always shown up
in places I shouldn't be
with all of my love

you can have all of me
just promise to be careful
it's all I have left

I built me
to hold you

she smiles
and I break into
a million pieces of haiku

there is no need
to chase the stars
my love
you are made of them

start over
as often as the sun
and love as
resiliently as the sea

love is free
to be what it is
when we are brave enough
to be who we are

I may never understand you
but I'd love to love you
while I try

I dream
of big sky
and her
under it

find her
wherever she is
whatever she is
find her
and love her
until she knows
it exists

some souls
are just
too beautiful
to stay

I love you
like I am a child
like I don't know any better

I know sometimes you hurt
and I know sometimes you break
and I know sometimes
there's just nothing
I can do about it

so I'll just lie here
and break with you
and love on you
until it doesn't hurt
anymore

I will love you
foolishly and without abandon
sometimes I'm genius like that

you were revealed
under old scars
and new wings

fly into your black wilds

dark nights
always shine
brighter lights

I want to be the man
who puts away your doubt
and assures you that
even your wildest ideas
of love are true

I believe in you
in every language

I've always been
a little bit broken
a little bit dreamer
and a whole lot
of hope

take me back there
behind these walls you've built
we can break them down
and be architects
we can build worlds
where walls don't exist

there is wilderness
in your heart
explore it
with bare feet
and awe

when she
is quiet
quietly
I love her

the ocean
does not
hold on
or let go
it oceans
like love
loves

she is
slowly undoing
everything that
has ever hurt

I loved her madly
so madly
she almost loved me back

we are all afraid
some of us just choose
to love in spite of it

I stumbled into her forever

this is what you want
right now
the way I'm inside you
hard and
with everything
I have left

this is yours
if you'd have it

I wonder if
she can see right through me
actually
it's what I hope

I can
only love you
as hard as
you let me

Scribbles

PORTLAND

often
the stars applaud
the love we make

but mostly
it leaves them
burning and speechless

how beautiful it is
when the lights go down
and her skin
runs into mine

oh how
her face lights
under the moon like this
my fingers
long and wandering
the courtesies
of her sundress
whose seams
now risen
high above her waist
offer a thin line
of wilderness
from which I
rarely return

be music
not noise
the world is
loud enough

what I miss most
is the urgency of her breaths
beating against me
like only I
could save her

she is fluent
in matters
of the stars

be still
the world is spinning
fast enough

we are all blind
if not seeing
with our soul

I don't know
words to explain her
just the way
the sun dances
on her wild skin
and the morning
moves into her like stars
and how she
always shows me
just how beautiful
tomorrow can be

the flowers are sighing
the waves are breaking
and it doesn't matter
who started it

you are so beautifully rare
to be built so strong
of things
so soft

I wonder
what it sounds like
when you speak to the ocean
and the salt soaks your skin
and the moment kisses you
like it will die if it doesn't

it's pride
not love
that fucks
things up

I was never
any good at love
but God how
I wanted to be

if we burn
we burn

this is what
fire does

when even the moon
has blushed
I know
I have loved her right

we were
always from
the stars

we break
in ways
that astonish waves

listen twice
speak once

I crave you
like morning coffee before I sigh
like that dream I can't remember

I will always be
a little bit crazy
a little too large
for my skin
I will always believe
in a love
so insanely beautiful
that it cannot be broken
that it will bring us back to life
back to ourselves
and back to the world
for which we
were truly meant

tell her everything
and you'll never have
to wish you would've

I stepped outside
and a ray of hope
struck me in the heart

there is no place
left to hide
but in it

some nights
rain falls
from the sky

some nights
it falls
for it

I want to
take a walk
with her

so slowly

it lasts
forever

I always get lost
somewhere between
her and God

thank God
one of them
always finds me

I am
the most terrifying thing
I have ever had
to overcome

what a beautiful phenomenon it is
to always be falling in love
with the woman
I already love

linger here with me
just a little bit longer
just a little bit forever

she started
with her legs parted
and her hair a mess

the moon and I
did the rest

it's where we all begin
in a tiny pause between breaths
in a clear calming moment
when we realize that
not only is it okay to change
but that the very life we are seeking
will require it

even love questions herself
and then chooses
love anyway

the world wore me
so thin
my soul had
no choice
but to
shine through

some smiles
never leave you
the same

every once in a while
you'll come across somebody
who understands you
better than you do
and if you're smart
you'll study the stars with them
before they leave

it's the human in us
that complicates things
not the love

and just before
the sun sets
if you listen
close enough
you'll hear him
whisper to her

there's no need to rush
we have forever
if you'd like

fight for her
and if she loves you
fight even harder

she arouses
more than
the morning

and to know a love
that for once
does not die
of selfish or lesser things
is to know
immortality

just her
and me
and nowhere
to be

if you have
ever died of love
you know what
it is capable of

the only thing
I expect
is imperfection
every last
beautiful fucking
piece of it

I stopped falling
for things that
weren't her

I was nothing more
than a twinkle in her eye
but God how I shined

she'll know peace
when you win
your war

everybody is down here talking about letting
go versus holding on while the stars are all up
there laughing at the notion that we think we
can do either

I come in assorted religions

be
too beautiful
to explain

be redemption
not pestilence

be what
your words
are fighting for

she's complicated, just look at her, mouth dripping of champagne watermelon and accent, the butterfly stalking her left knee, and how every star in every constellation has been waiting its entire life for this single moment to glimpse it all

love her
before
he does

I waited for silence. It rolled in like a sunset, always. I was accustomed to the cold and the brittle and how the seasons and the days and the years shifted like tectonic plates below our simple human feet, but it never stopped amazing me, her cycle, how it always balanced mine, and how despite it all, she always knew when to rise. That was when her words would rain, and again, I would be nourished and alive.

my mind is chaos
but it's beautiful in there
it's like nebulas and comets
and Chopin playing chopsticks
while talking philosophy
with the stars

even the moon
begins again
when it has become
too full of itself

I'm fascinated
with her mind
and the butterflies
that live there

All I've ever truly wanted in this life is for my soul to have left the slightest imprint upon another's, for my heart to have been loved for what's below my skin, and to know that I didn't compromise that for which I believed in. For my name to have been whispered, even once, and in this context, would surely mean my soul's freedom in the next.

I love when
she is all clingy
and up in my face

as if I
could ever breathe
without her

I love how the moon
falls asleep
so peacefully in her arms
it almost forgets
the night is here

and when she cried
I cried
and the world
smelled like rain

she smiled
and I realized
what I had been fighting
my entire life for

it's not that complicated
live light, love hard,
and always, always
meditate

we were always clumsy
fumbling around with things like love
and the weight of the world

I may never understand you
but I will always try to
I will listen to you
and I will never tell you
that you are wrong
for the only thing
I have become certain of
in this life
is that I am
not always right

I saw her
and forgot how
to look away

every morning
she reminds me
what it feels like
to fall in love

and every night
I hope I
have done her
the same

love them
and if they are hurting
love them even more

SAN FRANCISCO

I spent the most
beautiful of words
behind closed doors
on the one they were written for
the one who is no longer here
the one whose ghost
I write for now

all I know
is every time
the sun rises
I look for
you first

we bare our souls
in the hope that
someone might see
something we missed

and maybe
the only ghosts
are the ones we become
when we stop believing
in our dreams

I'll never forget
how beautifully she loved me
like I almost deserved it

we weren't two souls
in love with each other
we were one soul
in love with itself

I've got things on my mind, like dragonflies and constellations, and how delicate your fingers are when they fall into mine and scarlet hues of starlit evenings rapture us like sky-fire, and we go to some place no one else has dared go because there's no way out and only the cosmos know about it.. yes, love, I know... I've got things on my mind.

We're the persons, the lonely ones, the ones who run late into the night writing lovely everythings and lovely nothings and holding our breath in the air like blue balloons remembering the green grass and the hand of the child that let us go. we're the persons who don't forget what happens after love runs out and seeks shelter in the storms of the past and cinders and kettles like the one in that cabin we could never quite build. we're the ones who once, always, and forever, are dreaming under a maroon sea of salt and jasmines and stars wondering if it will always be like this.. yes, we're those ones.

And if I were to say I loved you, that I have never met someone like you, that my heart is gentle and open with you, that my mind grows wild and explodes like cherry blossoms with you, that every child in me has his first crush on you, that I'm in awe of every delicate gesture and motion your soul makes, that you literally leave me speechless.. if I were to say this to you, would you understand me? Would you know how to swim in this ocean?

some nights
I would fall asleep
staring up at the moon

other nights
I would almost forget
she left

she told me
I had a poet's eyes
and I wasn't sure
whether to smile
or cry

LOS ANGELES

and maybe that's the problem
even forever knows
I'll be waiting

a man full of sounds
walked into a world
just to hear them

I am never home
until her hands
are on my face

and maybe all
anyone ever really needs
is a few stars
a mountain top
and the love
of another

all she ever
wanted to do
was leave me speechless

and God she was good at it

let's just
start anywhere
and never end

take my hand
we can go chase the stars
and fall madly in love
along the way

she speaks
half ocean half God
and I've never understood
anything so clearly

I wanted to be wanted
maybe it was unhealthy
or maybe it was just human

and when we came
the morning came with us

Some of the most beautiful conversations I've ever had were with strangers I'll probably never see again, and I think in part, that that's what allowed them to be so vulnerably beautiful.

It seems some of us spend an entire lifetime searching for things we may never find, and while many close to us may never understand this, in our heart of hearts, we know that it's necessary to clear a path for the ones who do.

rise
be grateful
and remember
the sun's burdens
are far greater
than ours

How do I write you more.. how do I write you better than this.. how do I write you deeper and harder.. how do I write you softer and slower and so subtly your knees buckle and shake.. how do I spell the words that make you blush and soak and moan.. how do I love you with letters and sounds.. how do I write you goosebumps and quivers when all I have is these words.. why don't I have you.. tell me where you are.. tell me where I might begin to know anything.

she's why
stars are born
she's why
we wish

these words
these beautiful little sounds
trying to make sense of love
trying to spell out things
only souls feel

God how I loved her words.. the way they would carry me over the surface of myself, the way they would lift me from the ocean's depths and feed me air, the way they would finish me.

It wasn't the cities I fell in love with, it was the journeys between them. The quiet train rides, the beautiful conversations with random strangers, the hope that the next place would hold the key to whatever it was I was searching for, but the truth is, I wasn't searching for anything except what I had already found: a few moments of peace from the dizzying world in which we find ourselves, a brief pause from the chaos, and a breath so deep that everything and everyone I had ever loved made sense.

sometimes
the most intimate thing
you can do with someone
is listen

there is nothing you can do
to make someone love you
either they do or they don't
and deep in your heart
you already know

I think about you every day, usually while walking to some random job in some random city, the sun beating on my face, my feet trying to remember the forgotten steps that brought me here, wondering what the chances are that we would ever be in the same place at the same time.. what the chances are that it would be inevitable.

And somewhere deep inside, we all wanted to be chased and pursued and loved, to know that of all the beautiful souls in the world, someone chose to believe in ours.

it's too late for us to be strangers

I see her everywhere
sometimes in the butterflies
sometimes in the trees
but always
always
in the seas

she called me Michael
and for the first time
I truly heard my name

TEXAS

I love you
in every space
the stars have yet to find

we tiptoed
over the galaxies
as to not disturb
the stars

tell me more, tell me what it's like when I'm inside you, when our hearts breathe on breath and then become it, when the rest of the world slowly quiets to a silence.. just to listen

and what are
God's eyes
but the window
into each other's

DENVER

all I ever
seem to do
with her absence
is notice

compassion and kindness
are hands down
two of the sexiest things
I have ever seen

watch the ones
helping those in need
and you'll never have to wonder
what angels look like

At some point we all hurt, we all break, and we all question things we should or shouldn't have done. But I beg of you to let go of the regrets, it's a waste of energy, and that's all we really are. So do the best with what you have, love those who are close, and be kind to the ones you encounter along the way. At the end of the day, we're all just a bunch of traversing souls trying to be human in a world that has become anything but.

Of course I miss her, but I'm okay with that, we've both changed and learned and grown, and we've both become so much more of what we were always meant to be. Love is not something that goes away, it stays in our hearts and resides, as long as we allow it to. And anyway, what could be more selfish than ruining what we've become by trying to recreate what we were. Of course I miss her, but I'm okay with that. It just means I'm fortunate enough to love her, and I've got a hunch, she is too.

and when the sun
sets like this
I'm reminded that the ocean
is not what separates us
but the very thing
that holds us together

some souls
are just meant
to have their way with us

I've always admired
the love of the night's sky
how it holds every star at once
and still gives them
space to shine

I've been a monster
enough times
to feel for those
who have yet to be

I have stacks of things
I shouldn't have done
but had I not done them
I'd have stacks of things
I should've

There's a little space in the corner, just between the window and the chair. Sometimes, it's right in front of me, and despite my most valiant efforts, I can't help but wish you were there.

we just stood there
in that ocean
smiling
getting wet
forgetting about
every moment
we ever weren't

I'm a sucker for dangerous woman
and when I say dangerous
I mean intelligent

you can keep your fancy words
I've always had a thing
for the simple ones

I wonder how her mind works, if it thinks like mine, if it imagines the same tiny spaces between our bodies, the ones we will tirelessly pursue, the ones that will become so small, so dense, so infinitesimal that they have no choice but burst into a million new stars for us to explore.

we just sat there
perplexed
me and eternity
having a smoke
trying to understand her
trying to explain her
trying to figure out
where we'd even begin

I don't know
where we're going
but I'm pretty sure
we're going to need
a sunset and a blanket
to get there

there's a moment
out there
where we meet
and I for one
wouldn't miss it
for the world

When people ask me how I'm doing, I usually tell them more than they expected to hear. Maybe it's due to the superfluous amount of self help meetings I've attended in my lifetime, or maybe it's just because as I've gotten older, I've come to realize that 'fine' doesn't mean a goddamn thing, and what a waste of energy that would be, to not mean a goddamn thing.

I always
leave my hands
right where
she can find them
you know
just in case
she ever needs
to come home

So I was thinking about you and your thoughts and how beautiful they both are, and I was kind of hoping we could go grab a coffee and fall in love or something.

It took me twenty-five years of drinking to realize love was not something I was truly capable of doing while drunk.

it's beginning to feel
as if everything
I have ever loved
is coming home

we've been here before
you and me
maybe not in this life
but we've been here before

I don't have regrets
just a pocket full of lessons
I finally understand

I met a woman in one life or another. Sometimes, I try to remember which one it was, and other times I remember it doesn't matter. Often, she poses as a butterfly, or an angel, or one disguised as the other, yet the same thing always happens to me, time slows, my heart beats, and I breathe a bit slower, deeper, my eyes close, my head tilts upward, and a slow sincere healing smile paints itself across my face as if she were in my presence again. These are the moments love reveals itself to me and I understand that she is, and that she has always been.

Something beautiful began to happen when I threw away that last bottle, something magical began to return. It was quiet, it was calm, it was peaceful, and it was at ease. It did not need to be spoken, but instead, began to shine from my eyes as if they had become a reflection of the stars themselves, like the obnoxious arrogance had been replaced with a subtle, unwavering confidence. as if the selfishness had finally run its course, and collapsed, and was giving way to something better, something like everything I had ever believed in, everything I had ever loved, everything I had ever wanted to be.. something that resembled love, or God, or the Tao, or enlightenment, or any other of these linguistic sounds we use to try to describe things our minds don't fully comprehend. It was like my heart had been reborn, like this new life was finally at the tip of my fingers, and for once in my life, I was not willing to let it go, and there is something so fucking special about that.

when there is
nothing left to hide
we are free to be free

Scribbles

And after seven years

I let her go

Right where I found her

In love with someone else

MARKET STREET

I slept with a woman in San Francisco once. I never knew her name. Sometimes I remember her face, and other times, I don't. I remember stomping my bare numb feet against the cold concrete that night, trying to get some feeling back, trying not to lose them. She was covered in layers of heavy blankets just across from me. It was Market St., it still is. It was only my second night there, on Market St., on any street; and my feet were frozen clear up to my knees. That night never seemed to end. I remember trying to walk, trying to run in place, trying to do anything I could to feel them again, my feet. Meanwhile, she just sat there, across that fucking street, Market St., watching, observing, waiting. It must have been, only God knows what hour, when she spoke loudly enough for me to hear. She was waving for me to come to her, to warm up under her blankets, saying something about, I was going to freeze if I didn't. I had a lot of pride then, too much pride, then, and I didn't want any help. But inevitably, it became too much, and I gave in to her offer, to her kindness. I got under those blankets; she even wrapped an extra one around my feet. It was so comforting, so warm, such a relief to be there, to not be alone. I drifted off to sleep, there, resting against her. She put a needle in her arm and did the same. Yeah, I slept with a woman in San Francisco once, I just never saw her wake up.

THIS

I just sat there, here, quietly, shirtless, legs folded Indian style. That was okay to say when I was growing up. That's what it was called, this. That's what we were instructed to do. That's what the teachers taught us. It wasn't part of the curriculum, I'm sure, but I learned nonetheless. Children have a beautiful way of doing that, this. And this house is blue too, like the one in Oregon. That's the last place I recall sitting like that, this. It doesn't rain as often here, but it smells the same when it does, like now, like this. I wonder if I'll ever be able to write like I want to, more like a writer. Maybe sharper, crisper, clearer.. maybe have some kind of underlying wisdom to share. Yeah, maybe I could do that, or, I suppose, just sit here, like this, quietly, shirtless, legs folded, not call it anything, and just enjoy the rain.

ABOUT THE AUTHOR

She called him Michael.

Made in the USA
Monee, IL
11 January 2022

88670060R00105